HEART SPRINGS

Jubilant Inspirations from the Spirit

By Paula Pollard Mills
Copyright 2008

Blessings to you!

Paula Mills

Jude 1:2

ISBN: 978-0-924748-62-2
UPC: 88571300032-1

Printed in the United States of America
© 2009 by Paula Pollard Mills

Milestones International Publishers
P.O. Box 104
Newburg, PA 17240
303-503-7257
717-477-2230
717-477-2261(Fax)
www.milestonesintl.com

1 2 3 4 5 6 7 8 9 10 11 / 12 11 10 09

TABLE OF CONTENTS

ACKNOWLEDGMENTS

I thank God for putting such lovely people in my life; He surrounded me from birth with so many truly great human beings. Something of each of them is in my heart and indelibly in my mind. I mention my gratitude toward a few of them who especially made *Heart Springs* break forth in my life:

> My mother, Pauline Crawford Pollard, a literal Sonbeam, who has always taught me by example to see and appreciate God's beauty and joy in all things, big and small, and to be quick to love, understand and forgive. She is God's love personified to me. Words are inadequate to express the value of her unconditional love and support, and all I have learned through watching her.

> My dad, J. C. Pollard, a legend in his own time, who lived a life before me of giving every day and doing everything with all his heart. He taught me to fight for what I believe in, to enjoy being used in service, and never to fear giving ... quite dramatic lessons! Every day I remember his passion for living, working and playing. Every day I

remember his love.

My husband, Don Mills, who enabled me to have space and time to pursue the writing of this book … always helping and balancing my direction. Our shared respect and honor for God's creations and appointments positioned me and opened my spirit to many *Heart Springs*. We continue daily to take joy in what we see, hear and experience, and enjoy learning together.

My daughter, Myla Daune Mills Pitman, who has been a constant source of learning, revelation and *Heart Springs* since her conception. She has taken me to new places in my heart and always inspires me by her unique giftings. She is a born teacher, and I continue learning daily from her.

My son-in-law, Michael Keith Pitman, who worked so hard to help us get so many projects accomplished before I could give myself to complete this book. God bless him and his many talents!

My precious grandchildren—my M&Ms—Noah Miller, Selah Michal, and Laurel Sage Pitman, who have taken me to new levels of love and taught me about ebullient *Heart Springs*. They continue to be a waterfall of God's love in my life. Their lives make fireworks in my heart!

My dear aunt, Shirley Crawford, whose life was continually a stream of love, encouragement and provision. Her courage, persistence and fortitude were a living testimony to all things being possible. Her spunk, energy and accomplishments amazed and challenged me!

My niece, Karen Mills Corey, who stretches my world with her delightful ways of traveling, organizing and creating. She broke me out of many boxes! I thank God for all her love, laughter and time. I could write a book on our travels. She broadened my borders and heightened my vision! I am so grateful for all she has shown me.

Dear friends, who become our chosen family!

Christy Wallace, for all her help and especially her firm, consistent, loving encouragement, direction and editing skills. Without her nudging, I probably would never have finished *Heart Springs*.

Jane Willoughby, who never stopped exhorting me and always believed in me.

Charlotte Bryant, who so selflessly gave her time to prepare this manuscript for editing and publishing.

Betsy Allen, who gave her time to edit this manuscript and who years ago launched me into the adventurous journey of believing the love God has for me.

Lynne Perkins, for seeing a book in me long before I or anyone else did. She invested years of seasoned, Spirit-filled, balanced Bible teaching into my heart, combined with affectionate caring as well as thought-provoking times that enriched and strengthened the foundation of my personal faith in Jesus Christ as my Savior and Friend.

Mary Alice Hendrix Hamblen, the absolute best home economics teacher in all the world, my spiritual mentor and friend. She has impacted my life with her infectious laughter and liberty in my relationship with God. The order, beauty and creativity she led me into while growing in Christ is a daily spring of usefulness and reality.

Clara Williams and Ethelyn Rumley, who so powerfully influenced my prayer life and growth through Women's Aglow as I served with them on the Board and was launched into wonderful years of growing, learning, teaching, preaching and singing for His glory. May God bless those mothers of Israel and their prophetic, life-changing ministries. May all the seeds sown in all those years become delicious fruit for the body of Christ! Hallelujah!

The Rev. P.K. Price and the Rev. Jeanne McCoy, who prayed so faithfully for me and who illumined and refreshed me by His Spirit which flows through them like a fresh mountain stream.

The Rev. Rick Jennings and the Rev. Judy Jennings, who called me upward and onward for so many years in the Lord, always edifying and enlarging me for God's glory. Their loving influence swells the kingdom of God in me.

My dear pastors for a quarter of a century, the Rev. John Zabawski and the Rev. Deborah Zabawski, who have seeded God's Word into me and spoken God's will prophetically into and over my life. They loved me unconditionally as they liberated me to reach beyond the walls of the church and practice God's love freely and creatively on people!

The Rev. Ralph Brown, who saw beyond my natural giftings to the spiritual gifting and made demands on places in my spirit I knew not were there!

Dr. Dale A. Fife, who so graciously took time to guide and direct me in my journey to publication, despite an unbelievably busy schedule. His books, *The Secret Place,* about passionately pursuing God's presence; *The Hidden Kingdom,* about the journey into the heart of God; and *Spirit Wind,* about our ultimate adventure, stirred my spirit profoundly and definitely spiked my *Heart Springs.*

I could never finish expressing my affection for all the terrific friends and family who have believed in this venture. The Lord knows every unmentioned name! Thank you all from the bottom of my heart. I love you deeply. ♡

Paula Pollard Mills

INTRODUCTION

As consistent readers and students of the Bible, we become cooperators with God's purpose for our thoughts, even our very lives, if we determine to live out and allow His intended expression of His way and His will—according to His Word. As we travel on this journey of life, we will find that if we are open to God, He will reveal Himself to us through every circumstance, person or thing that crosses our path—good or bad. As fresh understanding permeates our soul, little sparks of enlightenment will enhance our relationship with God through Jesus, as the Holy Spirit downloads perception and erupts insight that we may have missed before ... almost like being born again <u>again</u>. Since I accepted Christ and was born again, I have known multiple times of daily experiences of God encounters, or of God revealing Himself or speaking to me in the most simple, basic things of life. I call these experiences *Heart Springs* because they have consistently gushed resiliency and new hope to me.

Interpreting all that is around us through God's eyes is a skill honed by renewing our mind to His Word. We become His effective launching pad for this interpretive skill through accepting Jesus Christ as our personal Lord and Savior. God sent His Son Jesus specifically for this reason, and the Holy Spirit woos and draws us to this. Responding to this call to salvation and taking Jesus into our heart as our Redeemer and Friend is the beginning of a beautiful relationship—a friendship. It's the start of a working relationship with God! It's the beginning of Jesus living in us, the Holy Spirit working through us, with daily "God encounters"— *Heart Springs*—for our good and His glory, bubbling up and overflowing in the world!

> *For God so loved the world that he gave his one and only Son, that whoever believes in him shall not perish but have eternal life.*
>
> John 3:16

> *On the last and greatest day of the Feast, Jesus stood and said in a loud voice, "If anyone is thirsty, let him come to me and drink. Whoever believes in me, as the Scripture has said, streams of living water will flow from within him."*
>
> John 7:37-38

> *My prayer is not that you take them out of the world but that you protect them from the evil one. They are not of the world, even as I am not of it. Sanctify them by the truth; your word is truth. As you sent me into the world, I have sent them into the world. For them I sanctify myself, that they too may be truly sanctified. My prayer is not for them alone. I pray also for those who will believe in me through their message, that all of them may be one, Father, just as you are in me and I am in you. May they also be in us so that the world may believe that you have*

sent me. I have given them the glory that you gave me, that they may be one as we are one: I in them and you in me. May they be brought to complete unity to let the world know that you sent me and have loved them even as you have loved me. Father, I want those you have given me to be with me where I am, and to see my glory, the glory you have given me because you loved me before the creation of the world. Righteous Father, though the world does not know you, I know you, and they know that you have sent me. I have made you known to them, and will continue to make you known in order that the love you have for me may be in them and that I myself may be in them.

John 17:15-26

"For in him we live and move and have our being." As some of your own poets have said, "We are his offspring."

Acts 17:28

Mark these Scriptures in your Bible, if you will, and let Him write them on your heart! ♡

Know that God speaks to us in multiple ways: through His Son Jesus; by the written Word and the living Word; by His Holy Spirit; through teachers, preachers, prophets and other people; via objects, nature, circumstances, signs, wonders, bumper stickers— whatever. We must tune our spiritual ears to listen and learn, and we must receive His daily encounters so we can continue to be encouraged. I write this book to remind you lovingly of His gracious communication to us all. I hope it will encourage you that God speaks to all who will listen and look.

Now, may I pray for you?

Father God, I bring these readers to You now. Will You please open the eyes of their heart to see You, Lord? All around them, in all they do … always. Guide their steps, guard their way. Flood them with Your wisdom and float them in Your joy. Stabilize them with Your peace, and clothe them with Your favor. Give them a hunger for Your Word and bring them into genuine Divine-exchange worship. Spout *Heart Springs* from the core of their being, Father. In Jesus' name, Amen.

Please know that you were created for all of this! Allow Him to bring you into it.

Finally, I have a personal request that you read and highlight this passage in your Bible:

> *For this reason, ever since I heard about your faith in the Lord Jesus and your love for all the saints, I have not stopped giving thanks for you, remembering you in my prayers. I keep asking that the God of our Lord Jesus Christ, the glorious Father, may give you the Spirit of wisdom and revelation, so that you may know him better. I pray also that the eyes of your heart may be enlightened in order that you may know the hope to which he has called you, the riches of his glorious inheritance in the saints, and his incomparably great power for us who believe. That power is like the working of his mighty strength, which he exerted in Christ when he raised him from the dead and seated him at his right hand in the heavenly realms, far above all rule and authority, power and dominion, and every title that can be given, not only in the present age but also in the one to come. And God placed all things under his feet and*

appointed him to be head over everything for the church, which is his body, the fullness of him who fills everything in every way.

Ephesians 1:15-23

Thank you for reading my book! ♡

Paula

SCRIPTURES

All my springs are in You, God!

Psalm 87:7, Author's paraphrase

...Above all else, guard your heart, for it is the wellspring of life.

Proverbs 4:23

The Lord shall ... satisfy thy soul in drought ... and thou shalt be like a watered garden, and like a spring of water, whose waters fail not.

Isaiah 58:11, KJV

The streams [river, KJV] of God are filled with water ...

Psalm 65:9b

For since the creation of the world God's invisible qualities—his eternal power and divine nature—have been clearly seen, being understood from what has been made, so that men are without excuse.

Romans 1:20

The handiwork of God through nature is to remind us of His sovereignty and love. And all nature echoes, "God is real!"

> *Praise the LORD from the earth, you great sea creatures and all ocean depths …*
>
> Psalm 148:7

Look at the birds! Look at the flowers! Receive inspiration from His creation (Matthew 6:28-34). Look at nature and let it teach you of the vastness of God's hand! (See Job 12:7-10.)

> *Do not store up for yourselves treasures on earth, where moth and rust destroy, and where thieves break in and steal. But store up for yourselves treasures in heaven, where moth and rust do not destroy, and where thieves do not break in and steal. For where your treasure is, there your heart will be also.*
>
> *The eye is the lamp of the body. If your eyes are good, your whole body will be full of light. But if your eyes are bad, your whole body will be full of darkness. If then the light within you is darkness, how great is that darkness!*
>
> *No one can serve two masters. Either he will hate the one and love the other, or he will be devoted to the one and despise the other. You cannot serve both God and Money.*
>
> Matthew 6:19-24

May we have eyes to see God's truth and goodness, ears to hear His conviction, and a heart to act on it and obey, that we may serve Him!

HEART SPRINGS

What are *Heart Springs*? They are an overflow of the heart ~ ~ ~ illuminating the mind and enabling a visible expression to emerge. *Heart Springs* are jubilant inspirations from the treasure house of the spirit.

Seeing certain colors or things that remind us of good memories can cause a *Heart Spring* of pleasure. Certain scents can impart a surge of emotion. God has made us creatures of response. He desires that our responses be filtered through His love and His Word so that daily He can inspire us and give us revelation of His truth and Himself.

Nature is His visible revelation of His creative sovereignty. To glimpse seashells of unlimited and awesome variety reminds us of the infinite power He has for individuality and beauty. In the same way He makes each of us different and unique, yet with the common bond of unity in His spirit. And even as the shells take on more beauty and appeal through cleaning, oiling and scraping, so are we transformed into a morally appealing and character-bearing people as we learn to allow what His Word and His Spirit say to us about our motives, attitudes and actions to change us (Hebrews 4:12). The God who created all is our Lord … our King … our Master ~ ~ ~ and He is in control of our life if we submit to His love. Knowing that nothing can ever separate us from His love gives me *Heart Springs*!

> *Who shall separate us from the love of Christ? Shall trouble or hardship or persecution or famine or nakedness or danger or sword? As it is written: "For your sake we face death all day long; we are considered as sheep to be slaughtered." No, in all these things we are more than conquerors through him who loved us. For I am convinced that neither death nor life, neither angels nor demons, neither the present nor the future, nor any powers, neither height nor depth, nor anything else in all creation, will be able to separate us from the love of God that is in Christ Jesus our Lord.*
> Romans 8:35-39

Are you experiencing the revelation of His truth that cleanses you from any fear, doubt or unbelief that would make you feel separated from His love?

He wants you to be convinced of His love, convinced to the point that your *Heart Springs* with spouts of joy over the insight of revelation of His unfathomable love! ♡

When you are truly convinced, you will experience "Sonbeams" from within and you will have a resiliency in living that encourages you and others.

SEASHELLS AND PEOPLE

Some of the shells my husband and I find are perfect, and they are a treasure to my collection! But even the damaged ones are special. They have a personality that is accented by their irregularity. Time may have chipped them or barnacles may have attached to them, giving them a mysterious charm of their own. Sometimes humans, in their efforts to be perfect in appearance, remove facets of themselves that really gave them a fresh appeal. A mole, an irregular tooth ~ ~ ~ sometimes such things can add to our look and make us more interesting.

Jesus rebuked the Pharisees for working so hard on their outward appearances and totally neglecting their heart, or internal conditions (Matthew 23:23-28). Being born again and daily developing our personal relationship with God will change our countenance. Getting things right inside will radiate to the outside (Psalm 34:5). Many times we patch up the external and let the internal stay sour.

Christianity is a matter of the heart, or spirit ~ ~ ~ it involves our having an attitude that causes our lifestyle to radiate what we believe and who we believe in. As we give ourselves more and more to the Lord, *Heart Springs* begin to bubble and we feel His power of love inside us.

His Spirit, like the ocean, is overwhelming, encompassing. We are the little shells floating in Him ~ ~ ~ He is in us, over us, around us, pouring through us ~ ~ ~ and we're in Him! (See Acts 17:28, John 17:20-26).

As the chips or flaws in a shell make me wonder where it's been and how it was altered, so do I wonder about people. What makes them unable to love or give or share? What makes them closed to God? Why do some seem not to care even about themselves? How can man kill man? How can wives and husbands cheat on one another? Why do families allow money or jealousy to split them? What causes people to become drug addicts, alcoholics, prostitutes? ~ ~ ~ Only God knows the real root. We call it sin; it is from Satan. But I wish we could learn to listen and help others listen without having to bottom out first. It seems that some of us have to completely hit bottom before we are open to looking up to God. Each human, however strange or mean or dead he may seem, has a past and stored experiences or lack of them that have programmed his basic responses. The greatest thing about accepting Jesus as Savior is this: *He restores our battered souls* (Psalm 23:3). Our past experiences cannot be changed, but our response to them can. He gives us beauty for ashes (Isaiah 61:3). He sets us free from unforgiveness, self-pity, selfishness, fear. … He heals our damaged emotions as we allow His Word to come inside us and wash us in His unconditional, never-ending, merciful love. It is bottomless ... unfailing, restoring, awe-inspiring!

Heart Springs that wash away trash.

Sometimes God inspires and gifts us at certain times by His Spirit and brings a particular message, word or prophecy through us to be spoken for others to hear. To have this experience or gift does not necessarily mean the person giving the word is a prophet ... it just means God has used that person for that moment to pour His word through. The apostle Paul said that he wished we all would prophesy or have the gift of prophecy because it speaks clearly to men and it strengthens, encourages, comforts and edifies or builds up the church (First Corinthians 14:1-5). Any word delivered by the inspiration of the Holy Spirit will build up, not tear down; and it will be in line with God's written truth. It usually refreshes and confirms things we may already know. I will be sharing several such words in this book that God has graciously given me at different times of meeting with the Body of Christ at church or conventions or Aglow retreats or meetings where they were recorded, thereby making it possible for me to share them.

God speaks to each of us in our own language and uses the things around us that we understand and to which we relate. My husband and I collect seashells, rocks and stones, so God speaks to us through those things. At one Aglow meeting, I used an enormous acrylic bowl, turned on its side with a net draped over it. I had placed it so that sand spilled out and large multiple shells poured out of it down the table in front of the speaker's podium. The ladies all responded very vocally and were affected positively by the display of God's handiwork. It was exhilarating and it made a memory. God used the natural beauty of it to inspire, refresh and speak to His children. I could feel His message bubbling up inside me.

This method of hearing from God is scriptural and powerful, and I hope you can receive it. The first message I will share I entitled "Seashells—God's Inspiration," and it was sparked by the lovely spill of seashells as a centerpiece at that Aglow meeting. I was asked to pray … and after the prayer, this word came …

Seashells—God's Inspiration

I have given My children all My creation of nature to inspire them, to remind them of My sovereignty, to teach them of My diversity, to call their sight to a higher conscious level of My creative love for them. Even as I have formed the many different varieties of seashells, so have I made My children individual and special. Some of My shells are large and tough; some are tiny and fragile; some are smooth and others rough. I have given some bright, passionate colors, and others neutral tones that almost get lost on the beach in the sand because of their pale, pastel earth tones. But I made each one ~ ~ ~ by My Word, in My way, for a certain purpose, a certain position.

Do not question My seashells; simply enjoy them, receive what they have to offer and move on. The spiny, sharp ones will prick you if you do not respect them and handle them properly. The smooth beige-toned ones, such as olive shells, seem to be more effective when grouped together with more of their own kind; but though silent and unobtrusive, they are almost indestructible in their durability and strength. Pink Rollers are so colorful and showy ... but they chip easily and cannot be crowded without damage. The larger shells are easier to clean sometimes, because their inside is open and willingly frees any residue or dead inhabitant that may be inside; their openness releases their decaying prisoners and receives appropriate cleansing that prevents obnoxious odors. On the contrary, the smaller, tighter shells are more stubborn about releasing their dead residents; the tiny inner chambers seem to hang onto the stinking stuff inside. This makes them give off an absolutely offensive aroma, thereby causing these shells, lovely in appearance, to be left behind by passers-by ... to remain as long as necessary on the beach to be cleaned by My elements and time.

Collectors use dental tools to clean calcium, lime deposits and barnacles from My shells for better-looking, better-smelling and more appealing shells. It is delightful to see how much brighter and prettier they are after cleansing.

Oh, My child! I created you, with your individual, special personality. But you, too, have deposits that need to be scraped off. Some will be worn off by time and the elements; but I desire that you, like the collector, take up the tools I will give you. Use the instrument of My Word, the power of My Holy Spirit and the love of My Son and allow Me to cleanse you and polish you for that irresistible aroma I desire you to have!

You were not meant to be left behind because of the stinking stuff that resides inside; you do not have to be left behind on the beach! Come! Let Me wash you in My blood, cleanse you by My loving correction and use you to draw others to Me! I desire you to be a beautiful specimen of My new creation, growing in My grace and glory. Submit! Receive! Believe!

Are you receiving God's inspiration from the surroundings He has given you?

He is waiting …

RIVERS FOR LIVING

Pat Robertson's son Gordon shared that one evening as he was admiring the moon and the stars in the night sky, he asked God why He had even made him. After all, God certainly didn't need him. The Lord revealed to Gordon that He had made man to respond to and appreciate all the rest of creation! God takes pleasure in our response, appreciation and gratitude toward Him. Wow! We have the privilege and honor of delighting God our Creator just by responding gratefully to all of His work! The Psalms tell us that an attitude of gratitude gets God's attention. Our praise brings His presence and causes intervention in the heavenly warfare realm! (Psalm 22:3) That is why Satan lures us to murmur and complain: It clogs the flow of God's Spirit ... it repels His very Presence ... and it hinders our *Heart Springs*. Murmuring and complaining are the opposite of praise and worship!

Rivers of living water are to pour, spout and spring from our belly, our inmost being, if we believe in Christ. These are rivers from within, the Scripture says (John 7:38). The source of this river is the incorruptible, imperishable seed of God of which we are born again (First Peter 1:23). The new creation we become by believing His Word (Second Corinthians 5:17, John 3:16) is possible through the eternal Word of God … our faith in that gives our *Heart Spring* the life of God. We can continue to submit to His Word daily, letting it cleanse us of wrong thoughts and unstop the clogs of His flow of *Heart Springs*. Hebrews 4:12 says that God's Word can divide soul and spirit. This is crucial because the soul is man-sensitive, but the spirit is God-sensitive. For rivers of living water to flow, we must learn to be more God-sensitive, more spirit-sensitive.

Are there logs, twigs or trash slowing the flow of God's river of love in you? Can you dare to respond to His unconditional love and forgiveness so completely that gratitude for His forgiveness to you would loose and wash away the clogs in your heart's river?

If you do, you will be more God-sensitive, more spirit-sensitive.

VOICE OF GOD

In the book of Revelation, John described the voice of God as a sound of many rushing waters (Revelation 1:15). This must be why we love to walk on the beach and hear the ocean. It seems to blow the cobwebs from our minds. ... I always feel refreshed and inspired by the ocean and its treasure of shells. I receive awe and inspiration from God through my appreciation of them. As I respond to God's handiwork in a grateful way, His presence blesses me with *Heart Springs*.

Rivers for living ...
God's fruit juice ...
Joy juice ...
Divine exchange ...

What do you call yours?

No matter what we call such a touch from God, I love it! It is the source of my resiliency in Him.

A lovely flower, a contoured shell, an unusual rock, a smooth stone or pebble … each one incites revelation in me.

All nature resounds with His glory! We must tune our eyes, ears and hearts to listen and see, lest we miss a visitation! When we take time to respond to Him, He will gather us to His breast as a hen gathers her chicks … and we will experience His very special energizing *Heart Springs*.

> Perks …
>> Peace …
>>> Freshness …
>>>> Hope …
>>>>> Satisfaction …
>>>>>> … Himself.

Can you hear His voice? He wants you to, even more than you want to!

Are you really looking and listening?

WELLSPRING OF LIFE

Proverbs 10:11 declares: *"The mouth of the righteous is a fountain of life, but violence overwhelms the mouth of the wicked."* And John affirms that rivers of living water are to flow out of our bellies (John 7:38). Our mouth should be a fountain of life!

But sometimes things seem to be clogged up; the river isn't flowing like it should. What is the problem? Whatever the clog is, the Lord has the answer. Psalm 147:18 says, *"He sends his word and melts them; he stirs up his breezes, and the waters flow."*

God has a remedy, a medicine for the clogs to the flow of His fountain of life and rivers for living within us:

> *The path of the righteous is like the first gleam of dawn, shining ever brighter till the full light of day. ... My son, **pay attention** to what I say; listen closely to my words. Do not let them out of your sight, keep them within your heart; for they are life to those who find them and health to a man's whole body. Above all*

*else, guard your heart, for it is the **wellspring of life**. Put away perversity [persisting in error] from your mouth; keep corrupt talk far from your lips. Let your eyes look straight ahead, focus, fix your gaze directly before you. Make level paths for your feet and take only ways that are firm. Do not swerve to the right or the left; keep your foot from evil.*

Proverbs 4:18, 20-27, emphasis added

Light shines in the darkness; morning comes out of the womb of night.

The writer of Hebrews said, *"He [Jesus] is the sole expression of the glory of God [the Light-being, the out-raying or radiance of the divine], and He is the perfect imprint and very image of [God's] nature, upholding and maintaining and guiding and propelling the universe by His mighty word of power"* (Hebrews 1:3, AMP). The New International Version puts it this way: *"The Son is the radiance of God's glory and the exact representation of his being, sustaining all things by his powerful word."* Glory to God! He has given us His Word, and it sustains all things—it upholds, maintains, guides and propels the universe! It certainly can be depended on to hold us! Jesus *is* the living Word! He is the power connection that is granted to us. He brings us our *Heart Springs*!

Do you realize who lives inside you?

COMING OF GOD

As we open ourselves to think about God's Word, His love and His gifts through prayer and meditation focused on Him, there is a God encounter. Oswald Chambers calls this a "coming of God." There are shining moments of illumination, of revelation from heaven that bring a renewal and a refreshing to our hearts. Everything around us resounds with and echoes His glory and broadens and deepens our ability to communicate not only with Him, but with others. All things become emotional word pictures or parables of deeper truths of Him. We learn to practice the presence of God ... to experience personally His coming to us.

Are you open to His encounter? Are you waiting and looking for Him to come to you?

A SHINING

One morning as I sat in my living room, looking out onto our deck, a spark-like star flashed on our wrought-iron patio table. I couldn't believe the beauty and fire of it. ~ ~ ~ Amazed and captured by wonder, I began to investigate the tiny fireball. Only about an inch in diameter, it blazed and danced, delighting my senses. I was so inspired ... only to realize it was a drop of water that had dripped down from the handle of a nearby mop! Sunlight had for that moment shone through the droplet in prisms of pure beauty. I was allowed to see a shining of God's glorious principle of light! Scientists could technically define the rays, expansion, and so on; but I simply received an awesome example and revelation of how God, through Jesus, takes us and shines through us at times to attract, inspire and reveal His love. (See Philippians 2:15 and Psalm 34:5.) It was a brief, quick moment ... a shining. It gave me *Heart Springs*!

I wonder how many shinings or *Heart Springs* we miss because we are too busy to look, wait and be still or available for a coming of God or visitation of His Presence. He has said He is Light, and in

Him there is no darkness or turning (John 1:4, James 1:17). Jesus even called us the light of the world! (Matthew 5:14) But how do we shine? Just as in the natural, we turn on lights by flicking a switch ... by making a choice.

Are you turned on to Jesus? Are you willing to perch on a mop handle like a raindrop and let the Son shine through ... to magnify Him?

BREAD

Jesus said, *"I am the Bread of Life."* After seeing the movie "The Passion of the Christ," our women's weekly Bible study began to take communion each time we met. The first week we launched using a prayer that hangs over my study corner: "Lord, make me like Your bread, Your body; take me, bless me, break me and pass me around among Your people!" The depiction has a picture of wheat, a broken loaf with the center pulled out and a chalice. The cloth under the elements is embroidered "I AM."

When prayed from the heart, this is a life-changing prayer. Think about it and you will get *Heart Springs* of revelation. What does it mean to be like bread? Wheat is sown; when in full readiness, harvested; crushed; sifted; packaged. Then it is mixed with other ingredients; kneaded; shaped into loaves; baked; sliced, packaged again and sold. Then it is bought and eaten, passed through digestive processes and out through elimination into waste and back to the earth to be part of the soil for another planting. The process repeats again and again … as long as the Lord tarries.

This is no superficial prayer; it is deep and full of meaning and commitment. Christ fulfilled it; if it is our desire, He will continue to fulfill it through us.

To be allowed to feed others is an honorable thing. To be broken bread and poured out wine is rich and deep, painful and joyous. It is a gusher for *Heart Springs*—the bittersweetness of a Christlike life that is ever shining and bubbling *Heart Springs* seated in God.

Our Bible study group brought the ministry Tablelands to Greenville to minister. The Rev. P.K. Price and the Rev. Jeanne McCoy came from the mountains to our town, and gifts of the Spirit flowed through them to us like a fresh mountain stream. The Lord gave this word to our group through Rev. Price:

> Your Father says, "From of old I have declared Myself to be the great I Am.
> All that you will ever desire or need, I will be to you.
> Now I ask you: Will you be My I Am?
> Will you say, 'I am Thine, O Lord'?
> 'I am Yours, I am Your hands, Your feet, Your voice.'
> Will you be My I Am?
> Will you be all I desire for you to be to Me?"

How does bread come to be before it can feed others? There must be a time for each phase of work. Preparation is necessary;

there must be time to plow, to break up the soil, to harrow, level and plant the seed. Every grain of wheat has its own place, its plot, its field. God will teach us where, how and when each of these is to take place in our life.

There are various methods used for grinding and preparing different varieties of grain, each according to its special use and purpose. The Lord knows what we need for preparation for His special use and purpose. ... Are we willing to give ourselves to Him, and to trust Him through all the phases? If so, He will make it all wonderful in counsel and magnificent in wisdom.

Deep *Heart Springs* are hidden in secret places. Are we willing to find them?

Will we submit to each phase of preparation and trust Him ~ ~ ~ no matter how hard it seems?

WILLING AND OBEDIENT

Years ago, the Rev. Samuel Anthony and his wife Rachel, who are from Africa, came to our church and ministered powerfully. One night, Rachel stood up and began singing in her deep, abandoned voice, ♪ *"If you be willing and obedient, you will eat the good of the land."* Over and over in a brisk tone, she sang these words from Isaiah (1:19). Her song was pure and haunting in its repetition. God's presence came in a profound way and a holy sobriety filled the room. Rachel's singing had a mystical African lilt to it, a definite beat or rhythm. I began to tap my Bible like a drum, accompanying the tune. At first, there was a strangeness; then our spirits began honing in on the repeated tune and on God's powerful words to us that night.

Usually verses 18 and 20 are used with this verse 19 in Isaiah chapter one. But for that moment, that night, the Holy Spirit amplified just that verse for us. God wrote it on my heart, and I shall never forget the melody or the words. God lovingly inspired, instructed and impacted us through this precious African woman who barely spoke English. The brokenness of her English, her simple boldness in repeating it in her rich, full tone—all of it was so luminous. *Heart Springs*.

Are you willing to be obedient?

CORN

While worshipping in church one Sunday, I began to hear a voice saying, "Aw, shucks! Aw, shucks! Aw, shucks! My people are tripping and stumbling over shucks and scales and external waste."

Then I saw a large ear of corn standing up. People were admiring its silky top, touching it and praising its silkiness. They were complimenting the rich green husks or shucks, speaking of how good it looked and how attractive the green was.

"I am going to peel you, shuck you, pop you and bring you to the internal sweetness of golden purity. Don't worry if even a kernel falls to the ground; I will resurrect a hundredfold blessing in its place. But do not tarry or linger among the shucks, for it will cause you to stumble … and I have higher things for you to walk in."

It seemed the Lord wanted to proclaim that the externals we snag on are nothing to Him; if we press on to focus on deeper truth and internal things, we will rise above any satanic stumbling ground. Often we are so taken up with external natural things that we are hindered from moving on into the deeper internal purity of God, drawing *Heart Springs* out.

May God lift our sights above earthly entanglements and even natural beauty, except to allow it to cause us to see spiritual truth and revelation. Ephesians 1:18 declares that our hearts have eyes!

Whether corn is dried, baked, boiled, roasted, popped or ground, it is good food. It feeds, nourishes and satisfies.

But fire or heat is necessary to make corn useful. Think about it: Sometimes we want to shine, but we don't want to burn!

Are you willing to be shucked down to the internal sweetness of purity without feeding the bugs of "But I," "If only," "Why me?" or "It's not fair"?

It is not easy. It isn't fun. But it is a God thing with hidden streams of life if we keep our praise rather than murmuring and complaining.

Supernatural living. Can you embrace it, no matter what?

WHAT ABOUT YOU?

The book of Matthew records a conversation Jesus had with His disciples. (See Matthew 16:13-19.) He was asking them who the people said He was. They answered, "Some say this and others say that." Jesus probed further, asking, "But what about you? Who do you say I am?"

Peter answered, "You are the Christ, the Son of the living God!"

Jesus blessed him for that answer, saying that man had not revealed that truth to Peter, but God the Father in heaven had revealed it to him. Peter's name meant "little rock"; but Jesus called the revelation knowledge of God "this rock," a rock of revelation knowledge from the Holy Spirit of God. He said that revelation knowledge is how He would build His church, and that the gates of hell would not overcome it! Revelation knowledge of who Jesus is, revelation knowledge of His Word, revelation knowledge of His direction give us *Heart Springs* and prompt the flow of the rivers of living water spoken of in John 7:38. That revelation knowledge of Jesus also gives us keys of the kingdom to bind and loose on earth and heaven.

What about you? Who do you say Jesus is? Your answer will reflect your destiny and where you will spend eternity. It will also determine your capacity for *Heart Springs*.

Sometimes revelation is called vision, illumination, understanding or perception. But whatever you call it, we need it to live. Paul spoke of revelation in Galatians 1:11-12 as he shared his call; a revelation of Christ as the Rock was given in Deuteronomy 32:4, 15b and First Corinthians 10:3-4. Jesus revealed was called the spiritual Rock. Are you building your house on the Rock or on sand? Matthew 7:24-28 speaks of wise and foolish builders and their ends. Our foundation is important.

> *For what they were not told, they will see, and what they have not heard, they will understand.*
>
> Isaiah 52:15b

Our daily choices reflect who we say Jesus is. What about you; who do you say He is?

Whatever your answer is ~ ~ ~ it is beaming out from you to others.

DECEPTION OF WORLDLY BUILDUP

Revelation is God's supernatural radar to get us through the fog of life! It is His secret agent against blindness, deception and lies. It is our *Heart Springs* of joy, peace and love. It is the life preserver of resilience against living merely by natural sight. Revelation is the sight of the eyes of our heart (Ephesians 1:18) that lifts us above earthly means and circumstances.

I use a lot of hair spray. I also use a small round mirror, about eight or nine inches in diameter, to apply my makeup. Once it seemed that my eyes were dimming. I felt quite concerned … but things became clearer when I looked more closely at my mirror. That morning as I was cleaning the vanity and larger wall mirror, I wiped the small round mirror briskly with ammonia and realized there was a clear film of accumulated daily hair spray buildup on it, blocking my vision. The spray was clear, so it hadn't been obvious that it was veiling the mirror. I couldn't believe how well I could see! The scales, or layers of spray, were gone, and I could see every pore on my face! My eyes were fine all along … I just needed to clean the mirror.

Just as the clear film had distorted my image in the mirror, worldliness and sin can clog our spiritual vision and prevent God's revelation from shining through. We need to be daily cleansed by His Word, and open to correction and direction for our spiritual eyes to see clearly.

> *For the word of God is quick, and powerful, and sharper than any twoedged sword, piercing even to the dividing asunder of soul and spirit, and of joints and marrow, and is a discerner of the thoughts and intents of the heart.*
>
> Hebrews 4:12, KJV

> [Christ makes us] *holy, cleansing* [us] *by the washing with water through the word ...*
>
> Ephesians 5:26

> [Jesus prayed,] *"Sanctify them by the truth; your word is truth."*
>
> John 17:17

Does the mirror of your soul—your mind, will and emotions—need to be cleansed from the deception of worldly buildup? Did you know that deception is a lie, and Satan is the father of lies? (John 8:44)

What are you reflecting?

DON'T FEAR—TRUST!

Sometimes fear or guilt can clog our *Heart Springs* of God's revelation, causing us to subconsciously hide from them … and from Him.

Once a little boy tiptoed downstairs after bedtime to snitch some peanut butter. He had just gotten a spoonful of the delicious treat when he heard his mom coming. Leaving the lid, jar and spoon out on the counter, he ran back upstairs and jumped back into bed. His mom saw the mess on the counter, cleaned it up and went upstairs to his room to find him hiding his head under the covers. She pulled back the covers and his eyes gazed at her in fear. He expected harsh words or a spanking. He knew his mom wouldn't like peanut butter on the bed linens ~ ~ ~ but she lovingly raised her hand with a warm washcloth to wash his smeared face. Relief gushed from his heart in *Heart Springs* as he realized she had only come to clean him up and tuck him back in, not to punish him!

Nothing we do surprises God or catches Him off guard. He is there with ever-enduring mercy, love and grace to cleanse us when we fail. But we must submit and trust His hand. We must repent when we fail. If we don't, then fear, guilt, hiding, repression and depression will clog the stream of revelation and light.

Are you holding back from His loving hand, fearing harshness when He only promises love to those who come to Him?

Just give in, repent and trust … you won't be sorry.

We must learn the value of trust. It abolishes fear. And trust comes with genuine repentance. Do you know how to repent?

GENUINE REPENTANCE

God has created us so that when we *genuinely* repent, relief and refreshing comes. If there ever was a time we needed relief and refreshing, it surely is now. Our world system has counterfeits for everything, and so it is our challenge to learn to discern the difference between the genuine and the fake. For example, diamonds are formed in God's universe by natural causes and time; but man has learned to counterfeit the diamond in such a way that it appears almost as good as the genuine. When we come to address the issue of repentance, it is no surprise that the Bible instructs us that there is a godly form of repentance and a worldly form of repentance. Godly sorrow brings genuine repentance that brings refreshing, relief, cleansing and peace— ending in life. Worldly sorrow or repentance brings misery. There is no refreshing, no relief, no cleansing or peace—only death. Our understanding of the depth and difference of worldly sorrow (chin-up) and Godly sorrow (heart-deep) is vital to our spiritual life and attitude.

Second Corinthians 7:10 tells us, *"Godly sorrow brings repentance that leads to salvation and leaves no regret, but worldly sorrow brings death."*

I am calling godly sorrow and repentance genuine because it is heart-deep. I am calling worldly sorrow and repentance counterfeit, because it is only chin-up—it involves the head, but not the heart. I have made a chart comparing the two types of repentance for a quick visual contrast, using David and Saul as Old Testament examples and Peter and Judas as New Testament examples. It is interesting to note that David was convicted to the core of his heart by realization of his sin and saw it foremost as sin against God and God only! However, he believed and trusted God's forgiveness: He *asked* for it in Psalm 51; he *received* it in Psalm 32; he *understood* it in Psalm 34. Then he went on to do mighty works for God. Saul, on the other hand, was only concerned that he had been caught and was worried about going before the people. He eventually ended his life in defeat, taking his own sword and plunging himself on it.

Peter, as we read in Matthew 26, disowned, denied and betrayed Jesus three times, but received His forgiveness and went on to do great things for God (Acts 10-12). Judas, however, also betrayed Jesus; but he hanged himself because he could not believe the love God had for him through Jesus was great enough to forgive him of his wrong. He felt he had to punish himself (Matthew 27:3-5).

I hope you enjoy this chart that compares, side by side, the differences between godly sorrow and worldly sorrow, and their results and consequences.

| GODLY SORROW/ REPENTANCE | vs. | WORLDLY SORROW/ REPENTANCE |

- Realizes that all sin is directly against God; is very God-conscious. Second Samuel 12:13, Psalm 51:4 David's attitude: "I have sinned against the Lord."

- Regrets the sin deeply from the heart and genuinely asks forgiveness. Psalm 51:1-12—David confessed his sin, begged for mercy and asked God to create in him a pure heart and to renew a steadfast spirit within him.

- Motives are pure and unselfish. Psalm 51:13-19 says,"*then* [after restoration] *I will teach … and declare your praise.*"

- Receives cleansing and refreshing; "*Repent … and turn to God, so that your sins may be wiped out, that times of refreshing may come from the Lord*" (Acts 3:19). (Psalm 32; First John 1:9-2:1)

- Believes and trusts in God's love, Word and promise more than in our ability to fail … grace!

- Romans 8:1-2, 35-39—David (Psalm 34) and Peter (Acts 10, 11, 12) lived on to share God's goodness; there was no condemnation. They believed the love God had for them to be greater than their sin and failure, and they shared the gospel everywhere they went.

- Is more sorry one got caught and self-conscious (more people-conscious) First Samuel 15:24, 30—Saul's attitude: "*I was afraid of the people. … honor me before … the people.*"

- Chin-up sorrow is more concerned with what people will say than with true repentance. First Samuel 15:30 says, "*Honor me before the elders … come back with me, so that I may worship the Lord your God.*"

- Motive is to save face, to look good. (We are not to defend or make excuses for our sin; it's no joking matter.)

- Never receives cleansing or refreshing; this type of person is guilt-prone … there is no joy and no love! First John 2:11—"*…the darkness has blinded him.*"

- Sees the sin and its power as being too big for God to forgive or cleanse. This person lives in self-condemnation instead of having faith in God's forgiving love. Saul fell on his own sword (First Samuel 31:4). Judas hanged himself (Matthew 27:3-5) They shared only their condemnation of self.

POWER TO LIVE AND LOVE SUPERNATURALLY! (forgiving)

NO POWER TO LIVE AND LOVE SUPERNATURALLY!
(critical, judgmental, condemning)

A Christian with no joy, peace or power is out of fellowship with God and man. What can you do about this state of affairs? Just get back into fellowship through genuine repentance before God. This is the God-provided privilege of being a Christian. It honors God for us to accept, believe and walk in the truth and reality of His provision.

Jesus Christ said that when the Holy Spirit came, He would convict of sin. When the Holy Spirit rouses one's conscience and brings him into the presence of God, it is not his relationship with men that bothers him, but his relationship with God. David prayed, "Against thee, thee only, have I sinned ..." (Psalm 51:4, KJV)

Satan's core project is to prevent or hinder God's supernatural love from flowing through us through repentance and forgiveness. But you don't have to cooperate with Satan! Short-circuit his control over your life—which is part of God's kingdom—through the awesome supernatural exchange with God called repentance.

For years I have used Oswald Chambers' famous daily devotional book, My Utmost for His Highest. I have stored in my memory bank the following things he wrote about conviction and repentance; I present them in paraphrased form:

Conviction of sin is one of the rarest things that ever strikes a man. It is the threshold of an understanding of God.
Repentance is the surest sign that God is at work.
Conscious repentance brings unconscious holiness.
Repentance is the bedrock of Christianity.

When we truly see the spiritual refreshing and energizing power that comes from our genuine heartfelt repentance before God, we will automatically flow in God's Spirit of forgiveness. First we take it inside ourselves, then we can pour it out to others … and He will be glorified!

Real Heart Springs. Spiritual power to live out His will. Grace and mercy personified through us!

Heart Springs of trust and relief , gratitude and joy. Jubilant inspirations. Do you need some?

GOD'S PROMISES

God's promises are higher, truer and more powerful than our feelings and thoughts. We have to wash our minds from all the world's cobwebs and allow God's Word to replace wrong thinking (Ephesians 4:22-24). Make the decision (Romans 12:2) to begin trusting God's Word and believing His promises and it will be like cleaning a dirty mirror: Life will change and revelation will pierce through the darkness, confusion and wavering that worldly thinking brings. We cannot hang onto both the world and the Word—that only brings instability (James 1:5-8). Just make up your mind to begin clinging to His precious holy Word and its promises.

> *For no matter how many promises God has made, they are "Yes" in Christ. And so through him, the "Amen" is spoken by us to the glory of God.*
>
> Second Corinthians 1:20

Are you choosing to cling to His promises over and above your feelings and circumstances?

His supernatural grace will enable your choice to do so. ... Did you know that?

Do not give up. Do not. Persistence in hanging onto His promises draws *Heart Springs* from His well of living water. Are you willing to let go of wrong thinking and embrace His promises with all your heart and soul and might?

COME UP HIGHER

God is ever calling us to come up, look up, be up above with Him. He wants to release us from the prison of the known and bring us to the unknown. He sets an open door before us and calls us into intimacy with Himself, that He may show us things we know not, that we may see what we haven't seen, that His glory may come in and go out in a greater way.

What we need is for His lights and perfections—the apostolic and prophetic ministries—to be enlarged. In the Old Testament, the Urim and the Thummim were used by the priests for God's revelatory light to shine through. Today His revelatory light shines through us. Do you remember the raindrop that fell from my mop handle?

"Come up! Come up," He says, "and you will see Me."

May we position ourselves to answer this call to higher life. We must be very quiet and listen.

Do you desire in your inward parts to come up higher? Tell Him ~ ~ ~ and be prepared to see Him.

IS HE FAITHFUL?

I have a basket of multihued glass fruit and vegetables on my patio table, to add color and decoration. One day I watched a bird peck away at the glass fruit; it would hold its head up, look around and go back to peck again. I sliced an orange and placed it on the ledge of the patio rail and came back inside to see if the bird would find the real fruit. It did.

The world has colorful counterfeits and alluring deception for us ... but our hearts are to be genuinely focused on finding God's truth—the real thing. He is faithful and will guide us into all truth and genuineness. Do not be discouraged by the superficial, artificial sidetracks; just keep on pecking, looking in His Word for reflection and guidance. He is faithful and will provide genuine nourishment as we seek, ask and knock.

A Word from the Lord

You have sung to Me, "You are faithful," and so I am. I am faithful through all the valleys and canyons and mountains and hills and ditches and waterfalls and rivers and deserts you cross as you walk through this earthly journey. I am faithful when you are not; I am faithful when you are not even aware of My presence ... not even aware I am there. I desire to exhibit a level of My faithfulness that you cannot see without walking in the hard places. Begin in the stretching places ... but as you allow Me to indwell you and walk through your house and all the places inside you—the secret places of your heart, the closet places of your mind, the library of your emotions—then the intentions of your soul, the fears and inferiorities and hurts and pride and selfishness, can all be circumcised and cleansed. Greed, control, partiality, even laziness can go. I will not only cleanse you, but if you will be honest and truly open, I will rightfully organize your house for your good and My glory. But it is up to you to choose your priorities and face your sin. Bring all things out into the light and allow Me to shine on them. Then I will not only cleanse and organize, but I will decorate your house with My gifts and treasures. I will transform you inside first. The outside will show it later.

As you commit to worship Me and not your own wants and desires, and as you begin to fellowship with Me, I will personally disciple you and equip you for life and reconciliatory ministry. The result of this faithful union of honesty and cleanness before Me will result in evangelism! The world and the church are watching you. They see it when you order your life awry. Repent! Open up! Turn to Me and let me burn out the unneeded, the unnecessary, the ungodly. And from those ashes I will bring beauty and order to your life—peace and joy beyond your wildest imagination. Don't be afraid to fling open your doors and windows and drawers and closets. Let My holy Wind blow fresh, pure, clean air through all that you are, all that you have and all that you do. My holy cleansing fire will prepare you for a higher level of life in Me. But you must be open and welcome Me. Confess … repent … listen to My correction and direction and receive the edification and revival you so long for to be the leader and follower I call you to be.

Do you really trust Me? Do you really mean it when you sing that I am faithful?

I AM.

I treasure the old chorus:

> "Breathe on me, Breath of God,
> Till I am wholly thine,
> Till all this earthly part of me
> Glows with thy fire divine."

"Glows with Thy fire divine" … Hebrews 12:29 tells us that "Our God is a consuming fire." We can note that there are two kinds of fire: The fire of hell that inflames natural, unregenerate, sinful man (James 3:6); and the fire of the Holy Spirit that drives out the fire of hell and replaces it with the cleansing fire of God (Hebrews 12:29).

Do you want Him to breathe on you until you glow with His holy, consuming presence? Are you willing to give yourself to His holy, cleansing fire?

LET NATURE INSPIRE YOU

My husband Don and I are avid bird-watchers and nature lovers. Seashells and rocks grace our home and yard, holding precious memories of times spent finding or collecting them. Birdhouses, feeders and nesting paraphernalia abound in our yard.

One spring we watched as a pair of birds built their nest, laid their eggs and hatched them. But we realized that all the baby birds were out … except one. Don checked on it. Its little head would peep out of its house, but it wouldn't leave the nest. It was tremendously hot that spring. As Don further investigated, we found that the bird's tiny foot was matted and coated in bird poop that had glued the foot to the nest. It was stuck, trapped in its own waste or maybe the other birds' waste, and it couldn't get free. Don surgically clipped the waste away from the fledgling's small foot. It was released! Such revelation welled up inside me …

First, I was so happy for the little bird to fly at last as its siblings had already done. The mother had stopped coming, so this poor little one had been abandoned. Its natural, normal way of leaving the nest had been short-circuited, but God had provided Don and me to help. It was an abnormal means of escape, but super for the little guy—he had another chance at life and flying! It is the daddy bird's job to come in and carry out the waste while mama bird sits on the nest, and the mama probably housecleans some, too; but in this case, neglect to keep the nest clean had snared and crippled one of the young. The nest, meant for nurture and development to equip the young for flying, instead became a trap. Someone had failed to clean it out and do his job. We see this in our own homes sometimes.

We are well aware that when parents don't fill their God-given roles, sometimes the children are damaged. Without help from the outside or the supernatural, the children cannot function—they are stuck. God's love is the reconciliatory factor that brings the help we need to properly function and be freed. Forgiveness, restoration, redemption, reconciliation … release to fly!

We were so inspired by this example to see how special ministry to those that are stuck can be. Thank God He provides help for those who are trapped. Have you ever helped someone get unstuck? Heart Springs.

Are you stuck? Will you let someone help you?

BAD THOUGHTS CAN BE LIKE SPIDERS
(Kill them before they multiply!)

I have a hissy fit when I see a spider inside my house. One fall there was a rather large brown spider crawling across the carpet. It looked bigger around than a quarter, but not quite as big as a fifty-cent piece. I jumped up and stomped it, squealing for Don to come. It seemed determined to go on, so I was forced to squish it by twisting my foot over it (dreading the stain it might make). To my shock and amazement, as I lifted my foot, oodles of little speck-sized spiders crawled in all directions! I was really squealing for Don now and trying to stop all those little living things from getting away. I couldn't believe my eyes!

Heart Springs kicked in over my anxiety, though, as revelation bubbled up.

Our thoughts can be like spiders. They may start out as only one, but multiply unbelievably! Whether it's a thought that brings creativity, imagination, generosity, Christ-likeness, worldliness, jealousy, anger, lust, unforgiveness, resentment, greed, self-pity or a lie does not matter: It will grow. It will multiply and bring forth fruit of its own kind. If it's a wrong, unhealthy or ungodly thought, there can be only one response: Kill it before it multiplies.

Paul wrote that we do not live by the standards of this world and must demolish worldly strongholds through God's divine power, taking captive every thought that is not obedient to Christ (Second Corinthians 10:3-5). This is a lifelong daily practice for active Christians seeking to live in God's presence. His Word tells us how to filter our thoughts and gives us the pattern in Philippians 4:8. Paul told the Corinthians how they could know the will of God:

Therefore, I urge you, brothers, in view of God's mercy, to offer your bodies as living sacrifices, holy and pleasing to God—this is your spiritual act of worship. Do not conform any longer to the pattern of this world, but be transformed by the renewing of your mind. Then you will be able to test and approve what God's will is—his good, pleasing and perfect will.
Romans 12:1-2

Please note that conform in this passage means "pressed on from without or masquerading" (see also Second Corinthians 11:14-15). This would be like religion or chin-up decisions; there is no heart change, but only hypocrisy. This is an external change.

On the other hand, transform in this passage means "turned inside out." The seed of God in us needs to grow, sprout and turn inside out. This heart change is from deep inside and changes motives and attitudes. This is an internal change, affecting the heart.

As a seed bursts open and the new sprout comes forth, turning around in its quest to break to the surface of the earth, so is the life of God in us to burst forth, turning us inside out. Peter says this about the seed within us:

> *For you have been born again, not of perishable seed, but of*
> *imperishable, through the living and enduring word of God.*
>
> First Peter 1:23

The account of the Transfiguration (Matthew 17) says that Jesus shone and even His clothes glowed. He was God inside and for that moment turned inside out. This is an example of transformation in its fullest. The computer term for this is reimage.

In Second Corinthians 11:13-15, the word "masquerade" or "counterfeit" here is the same Greek word translated in Romans 12 as "conform" (changes himself). The King James translates this, "be ye transformed by the renewing of your mind" (v. 2); this may seem to imply that we are to transform ourselves, but that is not possible. We cannot transform ourselves; that is a work that only God can do. We can conform ourselves, but only God can come inside us to provide the transforming power to change us ~ ~ ~ to reimage us in His image!

We are all up against the problem of discerning the real versus the counterfeit, of seeking truth in our deceptive world. We seek truth in our inward being, not just acting as though something had changed. The internal can become external, but the external cannot become internal. We must be born again from the heart, not just by mental assent.

Being born again by asking Jesus to come live inside us gives us the way to know the difference between good and evil, right and wrong. First Peter 1:23 affirms that we are born again of the incorruptible, imperishable, eternal seed of God. Inside that seed is everything we need to be who He has called us to be. Our daily choices either release the life of God in transformation or clog that life within. We should be aggressively squashing all negative, evil thoughts that enter our minds as if they were spiders! Replace that space with God's thoughts as revealed in His incorruptible, imperishable, unfading, eternal Word. Don't allow the world, yourself or Satan to set up cobwebs in your mind. Flood it with the light of God's Word and bask in His presence worshipping Him, listening for His voice and His direction.

Great peace follows.

Good fruit comes of it.

God's breath, His precious Holy Spirit, is a supernaturally refreshing insect repellent!

His Holy Spirit will bear witness with our spirit … we can follow the peace of God and reject what disrupts our conscience of peace. This is a spiritual boost to Heart Springs.

Are there some strongholds in your mind, wrong thoughts that need to be replaced with right thoughts?

The seat of God's throne and authority in an individual is that person's conscience. God's truth comes into our lives and shapes our conscience so that everything we think and do is "yes" or "no" based on Scripture. I am calling wrong thoughts those that are not in line with Scripture and right thoughts those that are. The level of conscience we want is to be convicted by truth cultivated by training. (See Hebrews 5:14.)

A person's conscience can be seared, evil, confused, compromised by worldly contact; or it can be pure, clean and clear through submission to truth.

Are you treating wrong thoughts like pesky insects or spiders? Are you killing them before they multiply and exterminating them with truth?

PLAYING DEAD

As bird-watchers, Don and I have had many wonderful inspirations and lessons in life from our small friends. God's Word tells us to watch the birds and flowers ~ ~ ~ to consider them …

A hummingbird flew inside and came into my kitchen one day. I caught it, but it lay still as though dead. I stroked it and prayed over it, but it remained very still. I was hoping it might revive. We made it a refuge in a shoebox, with greens for oxygen and holes for air. I put a blossom on its beak for nourishment. I placed it out on the patio, then came back in a few minutes to check on it. The hummingbird was gone! I did some research and learned that its defense mechanism was to play dead when an enemy was present. How does this apply to us? Well, Romans 6:11 tells us to count ourselves dead to sin, but alive to God in Christ. We need to "play dead" when sin tries to entangle us … we can simply refuse to respond to it. Think of God's Word and purpose to follow only that … not our flesh, our selfish nature or the devil! Even Satan would rather hang around responders. Nobody wastes much time on something dead.

We can choose what we are dead to. We choose what we'll ignore or resist, and we choose what we embrace, feed and nourish. Unconsciously, we are making choices every minute; those choices are either conforming us to the world or transforming us in Christ.

Be alive unto Jesus! Be active in allowing Him to work through you!

Heart Springs are waiting! Are you pursuing them?

DON'T RESIST GOD'S HELP—RESIST SATAN!

Sometimes birds fly into our garage. Then they can't find their way out because they fly too high into the room. One day one got caught behind the freezer as Don was using a butterfly net to try to guide it lower to fly out. He tried hard to coax the bird from behind the freezer to freedom; but it was so scared that it wouldn't come out. Sadly, the bird died.

Sometimes we fly too high in our own effort and knowledge … and instead of humbling ourselves before God and resisting the devil, we resist His help.

Is there some stronghold we may be hiding behind? Are we imprisoned by some sin that could bring death if we don't submit to receiving help?

We're just a decision away from being set free. Just a choice away from Heart Springs.

Are we resisting the right things?

75

DON'T WORRY, LITTLE PANSIES!

One day while Don and I were grocery shopping, some store employees were outside the shop arranging bedding plants. A new shipment was due to arrive, so the staff was going to discard all the remaining, wilting pansies. Hot weather was on the way in, so pansies were on the way out. The blooms were yellow with black centers and looked like little faces. I asked how much they were and the employee said I could have them—I would be doing her a favor to take all of them! I was so excited that I called several people to let them know about the offer. They came to get some too. The plants were straggly, but still had potential if given the right treatment. We brought some home, where I pruned all the broken shoots, plucked all the dead heads and planted the flowers. I gave them a big shot of plant food and water … and my deck became a lovely pansy garden.

Even as the knowledge of how to revive plants works life, so God knows what we need in order to revive. We may need some pruning, some plucking off of dead heads, even a little plant food from the Holy Spirit. But He knows what we need and how to revive us when we look and feel wilted. We may be so ugly that others would even want to throw us away. But not God. He always saves. He restores, forgives, renews—He makes us look good again, inside and out. I was horrified to think the store would throw away those little pansies. Why? Because I had hope for their future! I knew others who would also take them home and care for them. The little flowers wouldn't have to worry about being thrown away.

God is hurt when we are quick to throw each other away—so quick to overlook potential, to ignore His perception of a life. We should be looking out for each other when we get straggly ~ ~ ~ we should be calling others to help and looking to Him for hope no matter how bad things look or feel.

I am looking out at my pansy garden as I write, and I am so glad I didn't let those flowers be thrown away. Their little faces are smiling at me and thanking me for believing in them. They're splendid! I enjoy watering them. They faithfully provide blooms for multiple small vases all over my home. They smell delicious and can also be used as garnish on salads. They are little blessings!

Isaiah wrote, "a bruised reed he will not break ..." (42:3a), and this passage is repeated in Matthew 12:20. During the time of King David, shepherds cut reeds and notched them to make flutes they could play. Reeds were plentiful. If a flute were smashed or bruised, the shepherd would simply break it in two, discard it and cut a new one. But our Lord Jesus is gentle, merciful and very perceptive of the potential of bruised things: He will not break and discard a bruised reed. He values us in whatever shape we're in and will save us, help us and restore us if we turn to Him. We may be in ashes, but He can bring beauty again; we may be mourning, but He will give us the oil of gladness ... and if we are in despair, He will give us a garment of praise. He does all of this so that we may be called His trees of righteousness, for the display of His splendor (Isaiah 61:3). God refers to His people as plants, trees, shoots, buds, stumps, and so on. ... I enjoy the parallels, parables and word pictures the Bible gives us.

It reminds me of my little pansies.

Jesus said we should consider the flowers and the birds. He wants us to allow these things, and all of nature, to turn our thoughts toward Him so we can use our focus to worship Him instead of worrying. He wants all of creation to direct us toward seeking Him and His kingdom.

Therefore I tell you, do not worry about your life, what you will eat or drink; or about your body, what you will wear. Is not life more important than food, and the body more important than clothes? Look at the birds of the air; they do not sow or reap or store away in barns, and yet your heavenly Father feeds them. Are you not much more valuable than they? Who of you by worrying can add a single hour to his life?

And why do you worry about clothes? See how the lilies of the field grow. They do not labor or spin. Yet I tell you that not even Solomon in all his splendor was dressed like one of these. If that is how God clothes the grass of the field, which is here today and tomorrow is thrown into the fire, will he not much more clothe you, O you of little faith? So do not worry, saying, "What shall

*we eat?" or "What shall we drink?" or "What shall we wear?"
For the pagans run after all these things, and your heavenly
Father knows that you need them. But seek first his kingdom
and his righteousness, and all these things will be given to you as
well. Therefore do not worry about tomorrow, for tomorrow will
worry about itself. Each day has enough trouble of its own.*

Matthew 6:25-34

I was glad to bring the pansies home and use the tools I had to save and replant them to be beautiful again.

God loves us and through Jesus and the Holy Spirit, He makes us all new again, no matter how many times we allow ourselves to wilt.

This inspires my heart with springs of living water. This renews my hope. This enlarges my faith. This pumps my Heart Springs.

How about you? Are you applying saving grace or saving knowledge to yourself or some needy soul or situation in your circle of influence?

MY SPOON COLLECTION

For years I collected miniature sterling silver spoons. They're displayed on a spoon rack in my kitchen. It was like a treasure hunt for me as I would go to flea markets, bazaars and yard sales, searching for those with "925" or "sterling" imprinted on the back. No matter how tarnished they were, if they had that imprint I knew I could polish them. I stirred through a lot of gunky stuff to seek out these little treasures. If I saw "925" or "SS" on the back of one, I bought it and brought it home, polished it and lovingly mounted it on my spoon rack. I now have a beautiful collection of spoons from all over the world, in all shapes, sizes and styles. Sometimes I recall how cankered and stained some of them were when I bought them. But the seal of "925" or "SS" was my guarantee of their quality and my assurance that they would shine when polished. Second Corinthians 1:21-22 says, *"Now it is God who makes both us and you stand firm in Christ. He anointed us, set His seal of ownership on us, and put His Spirit in our hearts as a deposit, guaranteeing what is to come."* Our part is to believe, receive and choose His promises above all else.

And you also were included in Christ when you heard the word of truth, the gospel of your salvation. Having believed, you were marked in him with a seal, the promised Holy Spirit, who is a deposit guaranteeing our inheritance until the redemption of those who are God's possession—to the praise of His glory.
Ephesians 1:13-14

We are marked in Him with a holy seal, the promised Holy Spirit. It's His deposit in us. He will keep us—it's guaranteed!

Just as I know the seal on the spoons guarantees they will shine, Jesus in our heart is God's guarantee that He will complete what He starts in us … into our inheritance in heaven! No matter how far we have to go or how much polishing we need, His Holy Spirit is our security and promised guarantee that we are His forever. Philippians 1:6 assures us, "*. . . being confident of this, that he who began a good work in you will carry it on to completion until the day of Christ Jesus.*"

The blood of Jesus, applied by faith to our hearts, washes away sin and cleanses all tarnish and stain of guilt and sin. It unclogs our pipes for rivers of living waters to flow, and polishes us for *Heart Springs!* Yes! *Heart Springs* will be a way of life for us ~ ~ ~ abundant life of Him living in us and through us. Hallelujah!

So let us be encouraged that His incorruptible seed (First Peter 1:23) inside us will keep us and will carry us into all eternity. Something that is eternal cannot be killed. So regardless of what we are working through as we are being polished or how lacking in God's best for us, never forget that His seal on us guarantees our inheritance. Realizing that will give you a grateful, secure Heart Spring. I love it!

Can you believe and receive from this truth? Are you benefitting from the spouts of joy this guarantee from God brings? The treasure house of your spirit has the fantastic, eternal seed of God within, which brings forth the life of God. Does that give you jubilant inspiration?

DAZZLING

While spending a weekend at the Emerald Isle home of our dear friends the Wallaces, Don and I were sitting on their lovely beach house deck, admiring the sound and all the colorful sailboats and cruisers. Kevin's flat-bottom canopied boat was hanging beside his pier in the boat lift. It was a white boat with a wide red band around it. It was positioned just right over the water to reflect hundreds of glittery neon-like lights! I first thought it must be covered with sequins; but Don said it was the sunlight reflected off the water onto the red band on the boat. It was dazzling … unbelievable. It looked to me like multiple little electric lights dancing and moving all over the red band. (The white part of the boat did not reflect that way.) As boats went by, the ripples changed the pattern of lights. They were heavy with light, totally covering the red band; I saw a blaze of light that slowed to scattered lights. Somehow the size of the ripples seemed to affect the density of dazzle. I couldn't figure it out, but I was so inspired. It was such a *Heart Spring* for me ~ ~ ~ I began to think …

Because the boat was still and was positioned properly, the sun was reflecting off of the water onto the red band of the boat. I had noticed that when ripples occurred in the water, the lights were not as concentrated as when the water was still. Now, water is a scriptural type of the Word. Red is the color of the blood of Jesus.

God's Son Jesus is in heaven but comes to earth to us and in us as we believe in Him and place our trust in His Word, positioning ourselves in faith (John 1:14). The ripples and waves of His Spirit affect us in dazzling ways great and small; as the psalmist wrote, *"Those who look to him are radiant ..."* (Psalm 34:5)

I called Christy to ask if she had seen the dazzling lights, but she hadn't noticed. Busy with their three children (who I affectionately call my "3Ws"), they hadn't had time to sit and see. To be still.

I wonder how many times we miss *Heart Springs* of revelation or illumination ... beautiful sights God has for us.

We were so grateful for this gracious opportunity. We sat, mesmerized, for over an hour watching the wonder. Then, as the time of day changed, the lights were gone. Brief blips of dazzling lights still occurred ... but not consistently.

It was a precious gift to me ~ ~ ~ like a kiss from God! I thanked the Lord for His graciousness moving through our friends to let us be there to see ... I wanted them to see it too!

Don't you just automatically want all the people you love to see, feel and experience *Heart Springs?* Are you walking in the light of the overflows of your heart that illumine your mind with spouts of joy, insight, revelation and resiliency?

You were created to experience this!

GLORY

The Greek word *doxa* is translated "glory" in English. This word is so full of meaning that I believe we will never fathom all of its fullness as it radiates throughout eternity, rippling out like waves while all we can sing or say will be "Holy! Holy! Holy!"

Doxa has many meanings, one of which is "correct opinion and estimate of." The glory of God is a correct opinion and estimate of Him. God is light (First John 1:5-10); the life of God is light (John 1:4). Remember the beauty of the water sparkling the lights on our friends' boat? The sun reflecting off the water onto the red band on the boat in diamond-like flashes is the glory of God. It is just one of billions of manifestations, but a dazzling one nonetheless. God uses loving symbolism and typology; the message of this experience to me is this simple.

The Lord has said, *"Be still, and know that I am God"* (Psalm 46:10). If you will be still, you will know. Now, the Hebrew word for know means "to inhabit; to mingle life with life; to have intercourse with." Knowing brings fruit. (In Genesis, Adam "knew" Eve, and she conceived). As I was in a posture of quiet watchfulness on the Wallaces' deck, I feel I had a visitation from God. God came to me through the sunlight, the water, the waves, the boat—all of it.

If we are born again—covered in the blood of Jesus; and we are positioned and settled before Him—open to be a receiving station for His glory (which is what He created us for, according to Isaiah 43:21); then God will shine His Son's love like sunlight through us and upon us … even more so if we renew our mind to the Word. The fact that the sparkles only shone and danced on the red part of the boat inspired me afresh to realize we must be born again, covered in the blood of Jesus by faith in His work on the cross to reflect His glory to the visible world. Romans 12:1-2 says we are transformed by the renewing of our mind. Without the water, which is symbolic of the Word, the light from above would not have sparkled on the red band of Kevin's boat. Even so, without the blood of Jesus over our heart, we cannot reflect His light to the world. Christ said we are the light of the world (Matthew 5:14) and that we are to position ourselves to shine! Paul wrote that we are to shine like stars in this depraved generation as we hold out the Word of life (Philippians 2:15). And the book of Daniel says those who are wise will shine like the brightness of the heavens, and those who lead others to right standing with God will shine like the stars forever and ever (12:3).

God's presence inspires, refreshes, reveals, illumines and liberates. God's presence bubbles and overflows with peace and joy and light.

Being still positions us for the manifestation of His glory.

His glory is His presence. His presence is *Heart Springs*.

I love His presence. I love Him. And I love the Wallaces for sharing this place with me.

A Word from the Lord

When I said, *"Let your light shine"* (Matthew 5:16), I meant My light in you, not man-made light. For even as man has produced artificial light through electricity on earth, so in My kingdom ministers have produced a synthetic light in the stance of using My name. Moses' face shone from My light and My presence, not from a manufactured, conjured-up glory. If you will let My light in you burn high and pure and bright, your dross will melt and My holiness and love will come forth in power and magnificence. It will draw and dazzle and touch the world by My Spirit: Discern, discern, discern the times; discern My Spirit; learn to circumcise the man-made glory from your life and remove yourself from its continual influence. Separate yourself unto Me; come unto Me and allow Me to purge your spirit and soul from man-made contamination. Open yourself to My correction and watch confusion and wavering leave your spirit. I am calling you to purification and repentance, and I beseech you to answer with sincerity and honesty for results that last. My glory does not fade in you ... it changes you and transforms lives! My glory brings revelation of truth. My glory brings reverence and awe; knowledge of My glory manifests victory over every sin. My glory brings humility and joy unspeakable! I have created you for My glory, not man's glory. My glory draws forth fruit of the Spirit and it remains. My glory sets captives free. Purpose in your heart now to reject all counterfeits of My glory and seek only My genuine glory! It will be your anchor in the turbulent times to come, and it will shine forth flawlessly to the world.

Can you meditate on these truths and be refreshed and encouraged?

ABLAZE

As I was sitting on the deck meditating on all this, I glanced down at my diamond wedding ring and a diamond princess ring my Aunt Shirley had given me. They were ablaze like the lights on the front of the boat had been. They seemed to move and sparkle more than usual as the sun shone on them. Again I was impressed at how being in the light makes things so much more beautiful … how it sets them ablaze.

"Oh Lord!" I prayed. "Please help me position myself where You are, where Your light is, so You can shine through me and reflect from me. I want to walk in the light as You are in the light. I want to reflect You and attract others to You. Forgive the time I waste in the darkness of fear, worry, unbelief, unforgiveness, selfishness, self-pity, criticism, judgmentalism, anger, inferiority and superiority, pride and darkness; because that is Satan's web to veil and prevent Your light from reflecting on me and through me. I must choose to be where Your light is. I must position myself through repentance, humility, praise and genuine worship as I live in Your Word. I must learn to be still to be ablaze."

> *I will stand at my watch and station myself on the ramparts [a rampart is anything raised up, such as a wall, railing or embankment]; I will look to see what he will say to me …*
>
> Habakkuk 2:1a

Dr. Dale A. Fife, in his book *The Hidden Kingdom*, pointed out that Habakkuk is watching so he can hear! In the natural, we hear with our ears, not our eyes; but in the Spiritual realm, God speaks through visions, dreams and pictures. We see His voice! That's why prophets were called seers—they saw what God was saying. In *The Hidden Kingdom*, Dr. Fife takes us on a journey into the heart of God. Through his gift of seeing in the spirit realm and his intimacy with God, he ignited the flame in my heart for passion in kingdom living. It energized my walk with God.

We need to look to hear. Be still and look … see … know … hear. *Heart Springs* are waiting.

Do you want your passion for Jesus to be set ablaze? Would you like to be a torch or light to help another find his way to light? What are you doing about it?

BELIEVING

When we see the glory of God or see what He says, we realize that sometimes He asks us questions—questions that leave us speechless. We may be in awe, humbled or even weakened at some of His answers—or lack of answers! But still there is an encounter, an exchange that leaves us believing. You see, it doesn't matter to me that I may have more questions now than when I began this walk with God. It only matters that I see Him ~ ~ ~ His work, His imprint, His reflection, His influence, His glory, His light. For it is in seeing these things that I am truly learning to worship Him in whom I believe. I believe, not because I have all the answers, but because I have experienced God and have seen Him with the eyes of my heart (Ephesians 1:18). But I must take time to look; to be still and know. I must posture myself to be receptive to His revelations and manifestations. I must also be willing to respond to both His questions and His silence with trust. I believe that as I venture forth on my day-to-day walk with Him, I may have unanswered questions; but I can trust that I am and always will be nourished by the everlasting, eternal springs of God. His hidden rivers of living waters fill my soul. Deep *Heart Springs* reveal that truly *"deep calls to deep"* (Psalm 42:7).

It is my understanding that beneath the streets of Shechem in the Holy Land, a river flows. Daytime activity drowns out the sound; but in the quietness of night, it is said the music of the hidden river can be heard.

Do you ever wonder what *Heart Springs* are hidden and waiting for us to discover in the times we are quiet and listening? Look for them! Are you prepared to trust and believe, regardless of any lack of understanding or answers?

SEEING DEPENDS ON CHARACTER

Jesus said, *"Blessed are the pure in heart, for they will see God"* (Matthew 5:8). Vision depends on character, according to this verse. In his ministry, Oswald Chambers emphasized that even though God grants internal purity of heart by His sovereign grace, our external life and bodily contact with others and their influence require constant choices. There are times we must touch not or taste not; we must scorn sin if we are to be in accord with God's gracious gift of purity. Purposing to hold all of our thoughts and acts up to measure them against Jesus will help us to align our spirits and souls with God. Our soul—the mind, will and emotions—is man-sensitive, and our spirit is God-sensitive. Keeping our souls lined up with our sovereignly-created purity of heart and spirit is both a choice and a continual act of personal commitment. But the rewards are refreshing and keep our relationship with God working clearly.

A stimulant to *Heart Springs*! Do you need one?

Toxic Heart Springs

Once God graciously grants us His sovereign internal purity, making us a new creation (Second Corinthians 5:17), the flow of peace, joy and love we experience will be enhanced or hindered by our external choices to either line up with His purity or step out of alignment and be dirty. Nothing clogs the flow of living water like a soiled conscience and impure thoughts. Nothing blights our witness more than behavior not in keeping with the purity God teaches in His Word. Honesty, sincerity, integrity and truth all keep our wells of salvation clean and refresh both ourselves and others. Lying, lust, cheating, hatred, jealousy, unfaithfulness and unforgiveness will staunch His flow of living water and poison our well. It will make us and those who draw from us weak and sickly.

Toxic *Heart Springs*. Bad stuff.

Do you daily realize that the blood of Jesus cleanses away all toxins of sin? Our own admission of sin and a turn toward honesty in seeing our wrong will position us to receive and walk in God's purity. Are you sincerely activating His precious divine exchange in genuine repentance?

God's forgiveness coming into you and flowing out of you to others is miraculous and invigorating.

Supernatural *Heart Springs*. Good stuff.

LIVING A LIE—HELL IN YOU

Jesus said the deadliest sin of the Pharisees was hypocrisy. In our day, maybe our deadliest sin is unconsciously living a lie. Deception is Satan's goal, and if he can deceive us into believing his lies, that deception will grow like a fungus until we believe our own lies. We must constantly ask the Holy Spirit to circumcise our hearts and souls and reveal His truth to us. If you are truly open to that, God will show you your blind spots and deliver you from evil.

Sometimes living a lie may become a comfort zone—but it is never safe. A wrong mindset ends in the spirit of the devil, no matter how saintly you may be. Wrong thinking, lies, anything that goes against God's Word ends up with hell inside instead of *Heart Springs*. We are responsible for our choices (Second Corinthians 5:10). And wrong ones can be changed.

Are you consistently practicing the art of changing wrong decisions so God can deliver you from Satan's plots?

RELEASING RESURRECTION POWER

The more I am willing to be corrected, directed and realigned by God's Word, the more I will experience His resurrection power.

The more I am willing to see my own sin and forgive others, the greater the revelation of His supernatural life that will be loosed in me.

The more I am willing to humble myself and exalt God, putting others first, the more I will experience the flow of His living water in my life.

The more time I spend praising and worshipping Him, the more I will learn about releasing His resurrection power for myself and others. It becomes a lifestyle ~ ~ ~ by hourly, daily choice ~ ~ ~ by faith.

What are we releasing? Are we releasing faith or unbelief; hope or hopelessness; forgiveness or unforgiveness; sweetness or bitterness?

Are you making choices in your life that result in a release of resurrection power? If you are, be assured that you are a jubilant inspiration to others.

STORIES

Stories create readiness. They can nudge us toward receptive insight.

Gary Smalley has called stories emotional word pictures and teaches that they can open our spirit's understanding.

Jesus taught in parables, or stories, so that people could relate to His thoughts in a deeper way. The gospels present the good news in the form of stories.

I come from a long line of storytellers and joke tellers. Our family loved to connect hearts, memories, laughter and life through stories. I have shared some of my stories in this book to help open your heart and spirit to God's truths. The stories help us to remember. They help to position us for *Heart Springs*—revelation, illumination, understanding or whatever you like to call it when a light comes on inside you. Sometimes we are so closed, so blocked from insight that we need a stimulant, a clog-breaker … a story that peels back the veil or curtain over our perceptions.

Jesus used stories to connect with His audience, to help open their hearts and minds to what He had to say. Read this passage from the book of Matthew; can you hear His voice as He speaks?

> *At about that same time Jesus left the house and sat on the beach. In no time at all a crowd gathered along the shoreline, forcing him to get into a boat. Using the boat as a pulpit, he addressed his congregation, telling stories.*
>
> *"What do you make of this? A farmer planted seed. As he scattered the seed, some of it fell on the road, and birds ate it. Some fell in the gravel; it sprouted quickly but didn't put down roots, so when the sun came up it withered just as quickly. Some fell in the weeds; as it came up, it was strangled by the weeds. Some fell on good earth, and produced a harvest beyond his wildest dreams.*
>
> *Are you listening to this? Really listening?"*
>
> Matthew 13:1-9, MSG

You may want to read this entire chapter in Matthew. You will hear Jesus' voice as He spoke so simply and honestly in stories and parables.

> *The disciples came up and asked, "Why do you tell stories?"*
>
> *He replied, "You've been given insight into God's kingdom. You know how it works. Not everybody has this gift, this insight; it hasn't been given to them. Whenever someone has a ready*

106

heart for this, the insights and understandings flow freely. But if there is no readiness, any trace of receptivity soon disappears. That's why I tell stories: to create readiness, to nudge the people toward receptive insight. In their present state they can stare till doomsday and not see it, listen till they're blue in the face and not get it. I don't want Isaiah's forecast repeated all over again:

> *Your ears are open but you don't hear a thing.*
> *Your eyes are awake but you don't see a thing.*
> *The people are blockheads!*
> *They stick their fingers in their ears*
> *so they won't have to listen;*
> *They screw their eyes shut*
> *so they won't have to look,*
> *so they won't have to deal with me face-to-face*
> *and let me heal them.*

"But you have God-blessed eyes—eyes that see! And God-blessed ears—ears that hear! A lot of people, prophets and humble believers among them, would have given anything to see what you are seeing, to hear what you are hearing, but never had the chance.
Matthew 13:10-17, MSG

The disciples asked Jesus why He continued to tell stories to teach about the Kingdom ~ ~ ~ and Jesus spent a long storytelling afternoon in an effort to bring out into the open things hidden since the world's first day! According to this paraphrase, Jesus said some people are blockheads—they don't see or hear a thing! He explained that they choose to be this way so they won't have to deal with Him face to face—or let Him heal them! He told the disciples they had God-blessed eyes—eyes that see! And God-blessed ears—ears that hear!

I want eyes that see and ears that hear God's truth, don't you? I love verses 51-52 of this chapter in this version:

Jesus asked, "Are you starting to get a handle on all this?"
They answered, "Yes."

He said, "Then you see how every student well-trained in God's kingdom is like the owner of a general store who can put his hands on anything you need, old or new, exactly when you need it."

Wow! This is certainly enough to make me want to know the Word—to read it, sing it, say it, pray it and share it every day of my life. The riches of life are seeded in God's Word. Jesus is the living Word. If I renew my mind to His Word instead of the world, I can think and pray more godly, effective prayers. He will use everything I see and every circumstance I encounter to teach me more about Himself … to develop my character and draw me closer to Him!

What a *Heart Spring!*

In a way, we could say *Heart Springs* are like Christ-awareness.

Have you set your mind so that you are aware of Christ in all you see, all you do and all you are? If you have, you are a regular recipient of *Heart Springs.*

CHRIST-AWARENESS

Oswald Chambers has said, "self-awareness is not sin, but it upsets the completeness of life in God ... self-awareness continually produces a sense of struggling and turmoil." We need to keep asking Him to produce Christ-awareness in us as we read, study and think on His Word. Chambers also said, "Discouragement is disillusioned self-love." We must constantly be looking for Christ and what He may want to teach us in any given experience. If self-awareness and self-love are given rule in our life we are destined for a dead end. These things will only awaken and energize self-pity ... and self-pity is satanic. When we are encapsulated in self-awareness, as opposed to Christ-awareness, we can be devoted to ideas and beliefs about Jesus rather than being in love with Jesus Himself. Christ-awareness will enable us to go beyond devotion to ideas and beliefs (which is religion) and become intimate with Jesus Christ Himself.

In Matthew 11:28 we read that Jesus said, *"Come to Me."* This is very personal, intimate and real. Remember, devotion is not a ritual or an activity; genuine devotion is an attitude. It comes from the heart; it is fed through times of being still and knowing God without a rush of busy-ness. Devotion can be known by a person in a wheelchair, a hospital bed or a prison. We tend to think devotion means doing things constantly for the Lord. But real devotion lies in knowing the Lord in our hearts. It brings deep inner peace. Christ-awareness is devoting our minds, hearts and bodies to putting Him first in all things, seeing everything through the filter of His Word and His love.

Do you recall the WWJD movement? It encouraged believers to ask, "What Would Jesus Do?" What a wonderful training step to a life of Christ-awareness! In any situation of life, to stop and ask ourselves what Jesus would do is great wisdom that could avert many wrong choices and selfish decisions.

Do you need counsel today? Guidance? Encouragement? Choose to focus on Jesus Christ. Choose to be aware of Him and of what His Word says about or to your situation. If you cannot find a passage of Scripture to address your dilemma, then find someone who can. Or call someone to pray with you and for you. Ask God to speak to you through whatever means He chooses. He may choose to speak through a child; through an animal; through a stone, a shell or a flower; it may be through something spilled or broken or stuck; it may even be through a person you aren't particularly fond if. It could be a sign, a bumper sticker ... or a dream or a vision. God can also speak through the imagination. There are no limits to His means of communication when we are open and intent to be Christ-aware in all things. These are our *Heart Springs*.

As we determine to press into Christ-awareness, we will be pressing out our self-awareness and even world-awareness more and more. We will be delighted at the capacity and potential for joy, peace and amazing love that will come in a life journey focused on Christ-awareness. Such a consciousness of the Lord is a basis for miracles, a foundation for a life change and heart change ... first in us and then rippling out contagiously to those around us. It takes time and daily, sometimes hourly, recommitment, regrouping, repentance and humility. But the deep inner surges of peace and clear conscience are more than worth it. Eternal seeds are being sown.

However, we may also feel alone or rejected, odd or distant in the world's kingdom, especially if we are in an arena of those who have not, will not and want not to be Christ-aware. Self-centeredness will scorn Christ-centeredness and even mock it. But we must be accountable and responsible to God's kingdom; we must prepare ourselves to know we are choosing to live for God's kingdom—for His pleasure, and not man's. Knowing and following what God's Word says and instructs me to do will rub worldliness the wrong way; it certainly won't be popular. Christ-awareness causes us to be more eternity-minded, thinking more of the long-term consequences of our thoughts and actions. Self-awareness is more about me, about what I want. It is focused primarily in the now. It's a difference of darkness and light.

It is important to prepare ourselves for this conflict. But God is with us, He is on our side and He will enable us to do what His standard calls us to. We can depend on Him; we can trust Him. To be close to Him and intently rightly related to Him, purposefully seeking and following Him, will take us into unspeakable, unimaginable, awesome places in His heart. It will bring us into kingdom living, where the very air is right standing with God, peace with Jesus and joy in the Holy Spirit.

Talk about *Heart Springs!* Thank You, Lord!

Let it be so with me and with you, too.

Is Christ-awareness or self-awareness the story of your heart?

DIVERSITY

As we learn to live in this wonderful supernatural kingdom of God, we must begin to recognize the diversity within it. God's people are from all walks and cultures of life, and each one brings a different flavor or insight to the kingdom. Each has experienced different levels of pain or joy, injustice or love. Some have been abused; some have not. Many (or most?) come from dysfunctional backgrounds. ... Some are from educated or refined backgrounds and others from poor ones with a lack of education. Some may be innocently ignorant, others hardened and not yet healed or freed from sin's mark of deceitfulness, dishonesty and manipulation. While God wants us all to be washed clean, it does take longer for some of us than others to surrender all and be totally freed. With that in mind, we must be advised that Christians are a work in continual progress, and some are further along than others. We may fail miserably, but our core hope lies in His ever-enduring mercy, His eternal forgiveness and the unconditional love that ever calls us back to Him. His love polishes, refines and educates us in faith if we allow it, receive it and surrender to it. The world does not understand this and sees it as weakness. Only the revelation of God through His Holy Spirit can properly reveal the value of the all-consuming love of God. It alone enables us to be together as believers in the body of Christ—His church.

First Corinthians 12 contains the Bible's instruction about spiritual gifts and the amazing sovereign placement and appointment of each member in Christ's body, the church. It addresses the diversity of the body and honors each one's purpose at whatever place we have been given to work in the network of body ministry. It names the multiple gifts and then emphasizes that none of the gifts is any good without godly love. Many of us wish we were something else other than what He made us. But whether our gift of service is a highly visible or a less noticed one, we are told to compare the gifts named in the body to a natural body. Maybe the belly button wishes it were a hand ... or the eye would like to be a mouth. But every single part of the body is necessary and is to be honored. Each has its desirable and undesirable facets. Our concern is to learn to be the best of whatever we are. That is done by searching and seeking out God's instruction on unconditional love.

Paul, in First Corinthians 13:4-8a, describes unconditional love (Greek, *agape*). Its qualities are stable, consistent and powerful. They are like lasers in our world, and they even give off an aroma! (See Second Corinthians 2:14-16.) The traits of *agape* love are Christlike. They include:

Patience
Kindness

Not envious
Not boastful
Not prideful
Not rude
Not self-seeking
Not easily angered
Keeps no record of wrongs
Not delighting in evil
Rejoicing in truth

This kind of love always commits to ...

Protecting
Trusting
Hoping
Persevering

These are the ingredients of God's never-failing, never-ending love. When we pursue and apply them, allowing them to rule and reign in our lives, the precious manifestation of the spiritual gifts will begin to flow from us like rivers of living water. There are more than just one of these rivers; God will use the Holy Spirit to pour through you whichever one is needed. Even though many people have a particularly strong gifting in one area, that need not be limiting; we are to stay open and free for His use of us as He chooses. He can flow as He wills through us (First Corinthians 12:11). Our concern is to pursue the godly love that is unconditional and never-ending so that our gifts will do good consistently, bringing edification to the body and not confusion or condemnation.

God's love, working in us and through us, never fails (First Corinthians 13:8a).

Could there be an area in which we may be failing because our love is worldly and conditional instead of godly and unconditional?

DEALING WITH SIN

How we understand or interpret what we see determines our destiny. God wants us to realign our focus through His eyes. Self-condemnation is neither productive nor healthy. In Romans 8:1, Paul teaches us that there is no condemnation to those who are in Christ. There is only correction, direction and edification for the people of God. (What a *Heart Spring*!)

So what should we do with a recognized sin in our life? Well, let's look at it as a splinter in your finger. Don't cut your finger off—remove the splinter! First align the sin with God's Word. When you see that it fails, admit it, repent and let the blood of Jesus cover it, blotting it out (First John 1:9; Isaiah 43:25; Jeremiah 31:34b). God sees you as His child. He loves you even when you have a splinter, but He wants to help you remove that sliver before it becomes infected. He will supply the grace, mercy and forgiveness to wash our sin away. Our part is to deal with it, treating it like a splinter; we have to commit to His divine work as He removes it … as many times as necessary. But we must also separate the sin from the sinner. He loves the sinner, but hates the sin. He can handle it. We must accept this truth by faith (Hebrews 11:1).

Is this truth a reality in your life?

Are you helping others to realize it?

REFLUX/REFLUSH

Sometimes a recurring sin or a besetting sin will repeatedly come back to us. We may wonder if we can ever be free … it's like reflux.

Our commode was having trouble flushing … stuff just kept coming back into the bowl. We would have to flush it several times to finally clear it. But Don said, "Just keep flushing it until it's clear." What a nuisance … but it would finally clear up if we persisted in flushing.

If sin comes back like a reflux to you … persist in reflushing it by faith in the cleansing power of the blood of Jesus. Don't give up. Persist in pursuing the forgiving, cleansing, unconditional love of God. Your persistence in repenting and applying the blood of Jesus to the sin will be a testimony that God's love is more powerful than your failures; your faith in that is appropriated by persistence in repenting and by believing more in Him than your failure.

I remember a line from a song: " ... grace that is greater than all our sin." Sing of God's grace—at the sink, in the tub, in your car ... just sing it out!

Of course, there are some situations that need special help and assistance, perhaps a ministry of deliverance and prayer. Don't hesitate to reach out for help when you are not experiencing relief from your prayers alone with God. We all need each other and God is pleased when we pray and work together for our own good and His glory. Sometimes multiple flushing seems to fail. Then what do we do? We call the plumber—someone specially trained and experienced in solving the problem! God has fervent, sincere, gifted ministers and helpers in His body to provide the help needed for His grace to flow. Do not hesitate to use them!

Is there a problem you have struggled with for too long? Do you need extra help to get free? God has someone to help you. Ask Him to guide you to the right person. He has some really great plumbers on His main line.

PLEASE KNOW!

God created us for His pleasure, for a divine love exchange relationship through reconciliation with Him. The Bible tells us that God is love and that His kind of love never fails. When He is accepted into our hearts, His love is in us and is meant to grow and swell and overflow in the earth in a healing, refreshing, reconciliatory way (Second Corinthians 5:16-21).

Please know it is the devil's intention to stunt, thwart and minimize this love of our God. His mission is to stop all flow of rivers for living and spouts of *Heart Springs*. We must arm ourselves with the truth of God's Word and fight; we have to resist the enemy's lies through faith, prayer and worship.

The worldly version of love is deceptive and conditional; we could call it "love if" or "love because of." Godly love is unconditional: "Love, period." It is eternal. Worldly love is natural and has limits; godly love is supernatural and knows no limits. To the degree that we renew our mind to God's love and submit to it, we will be able to give it out to others. This is the ministry of reconciliation. Our families, our friends, our church and the whole world are in desperate need of seeing someone really live out this kind of love and commit to practicing it on each other.

Did you know you can make a difference in your world by learning to love in God's way and allowing it to erupt and overflow? Did you know learning to love in God's way will bring jubilant inspirations from the treasure house of your spirit? *Heart Springs!*

Please know.

Paula Pollard Mills has been married to her husband Don for 44 *years*. He is now a freelance photographer and a retired Fire Battalion Chief. They live in Greenville, N.C., where they were both born. A home economics major at East Carolina University, Paula is a semi-retired interior decorator. She believes deeply that our homes are spiritual launching pads for ministry. She and Don have one daughter and three grandchildren.

Over the past 30 years, Paula has enjoyed ministering through speaking, singing, teaching, preaching, drama and decorating at various retreats, conventions, seminars, workshops and churches as well as Women's Aglow chapters across North Carolina. In her twentieth year of teaching weekly Bible study, she teaches women, couples and children; she also teaches at a women's prison ministry. She and Don enjoy mentoring at large in the body of Christ.

Paula has a passion for sharing God's Word with others because of all it has meant to her. This is her first book, and she hopes it may spark *Heart Springs* in you!

Have you ever wished God would speak to you? Have you wondered what He might say? Then it's time to start looking for *Heart Springs*. Join author and Bible teacher Paula Pollard Mills as she launches you on a journey into hearing God for yourself. Recounting many instances of hearing from God in everyday life, Mills shows how your spirit can bubble up with *Heart Springs*— touches from God that fill your spirit and overflow to others.

Has God ever spoken to you through the reflection of light on a boat? Has He revealed Himself through a drop of water splashing down from a mop handle? How about through a tiny hummingbird or a lovely seashell? In *Heart Springs*, Bible teacher and author Paula Pollard Mills shows how God has spoken to her ... and how He can speak to you. Mills shares how she finds God in everyday life and shares how you, too, can experience Heart Springs—touches from God that lift and encourage your spirit.

Paula P. Mills
507 Highland Avenue
Greenville, N. C. 27858
email: pmills45@yahoo.com

Oswald Chambers, My Utmost for His Highest (Grand Rapids, MI: Discovery House Publishers, 1992).

"Breathe on Me, Breath of God," v. 3. Edwin Hatch and Robert Jackson.

Dr. Dale A. Fife, The Hidden Kingdom (New Kensington, PA : Whitaker House, 2003).

Oswald Chambers, My Utmost for His Highest (Grand Rapids, MI: Discovery House Publishers, 1992).

Ibid.

GODLY SORROW/ REPENTANCE	vs.	WORLDLY SORROW/ REPENTANCE

• Realizes that all sin is directly against God; is very God-conscious. Second Samuel 12:13, Psalm 51:4 David's attitude: "I have sinned against the Lord."	• Is more sorry one got caught and self-conscious (more people-conscious) First Samuel 15:24, 30—Saul's attitude: *"I was afraid of the people. ... honor me before ... the people."*
• Regrets the sin deeply from the heart and genuinely asks forgiveness. Psalm 51:1-12—David confessed his sin, begged for mercy and asked God to create in him a pure heart and to renew a steadfast spirit within him.	• Chin-up sorrow is more concerned with what people will say than with true repentance. First Samuel 15:30 says, *"Honor me before the elders ... come back with me, so that I may worship the Lord your God."*
• Motives are pure and unselfish. Psalm 51:13-19 says,*"then* [after restoration] *I will teach ... and declare your praise."*	• Motive is to save face, to look good. (We are not to defend or make excuses for our sin; it's no joking matter.)
• Receives cleansing and refreshing; *"Repent ... and turn to God, so that your sins may be wiped out, that times of refreshing may come from the Lord"* (Acts 3:19). (Psalm 32; First John 1:9-2:1)	• Never receives cleansing or refreshing; this type of person is guilt-prone ... there is no joy and no love! First John 2:11—*"...the darkness has blinded him."*
• Believes and trusts in God's love, Word and promise more than in our ability to fail ... grace!	• Sees the sin and its power as being too big for God to forgive or cleanse. This person lives in self-condemnation instead of having faith in God's forgiving love. Saul fell on his own sword (First Samuel 31:4). Judas hanged himself (Matthew 27:3-5) They shared only their condemnation of self.
• Romans 8:1-2, 35-39—David (Psalm 34) and Peter (Acts 10, 11, 12) lived on to share God's goodness; there was no condemnation. They believed the love God had for them to be greater than their sin and failure, and they shared the gospel everywhere they went.	

POWER TO LIVE AND LOVE SUPERNATURALLY! (forgiving)	**NO POWER TO LIVE AND LOVE SUPERNATURALLY!** (critical, judgmental, condemning)

GODLY SORROW/ REPENTANCE	vs.	WORLDLY SORROW/ REPENTANCE

GODLY SORROW/ REPENTANCE	WORLDLY SORROW/ REPENTANCE
• Realizes that all sin is directly against God; is very God-conscious. Second Samuel 12:13, Psalm 51:4 David's attitude: "I have sinned against the Lord."	• Is more sorry one got caught and self-conscious (more people-conscious) First Samuel 15:24, 30—Saul's attitude: "I was afraid of the people. ... honor me before ... the people."
• Regrets the sin deeply from the heart and genuinely asks forgiveness. Psalm 51:1-12—David confessed his sin, begged for mercy and asked God to create in him a pure heart and to renew a steadfast spirit within him.	• Chin-up sorrow is more concerned with what people will say than with true repentance. First Samuel 15:30 says, "Honor me before the elders ... come back with me, so that I may worship the Lord your God."
• Motives are pure and unselfish. Psalm 51:13-19 says,"then [after restoration] I will teach ... and declare your praise."	• Motive is to save face, to look good. (We are not to defend or make excuses for our sin; it's no joking matter.)
• Receives cleansing and refreshing; "Repent ... and turn to God, so that your sins may be wiped out, that times of refreshing may come from the Lord" (Acts 3:19). (Psalm 32; First John 1:9-2:1)	• Never receives cleansing or refreshing; this type of person is guilt-prone ... there is no joy and no love! First John 2:11—"...the darkness has blinded him."
• Believes and trusts in God's love, Word and promise more than in our ability to fail ... grace!	• Sees the sin and its power as being too big for God to forgive or cleanse. This person lives in self-condemnation instead of having faith in God's forgiving love. Saul fell on his own sword (First Samuel 31:4). Judas hanged himself (Matthew 27:3-5) They shared only their condemnation of self.
• Romans 8:1-2, 35-39—David (Psalm 34) and Peter (Acts 10, 11, 12) lived on to share God's goodness; there was no condemnation. They believed the love God had for them to be greater than their sin and failure, and they shared the gospel everywhere they went.	

POWER TO LIVE AND LOVE SUPERNATURALLY! (forgiving)

NO POWER TO LIVE AND LOVE SUPERNATURALLY!
(critical, judgmental, condemning)

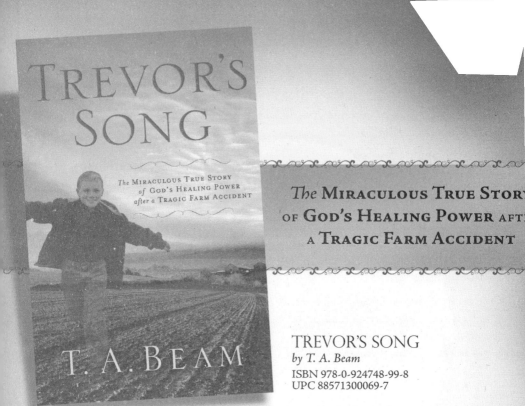